POSITIVE PEOPLE LEADERSHIP

POSITIVE

PEOPLE

LEADERSHIP

Fifty ways to create fulfilling
and enjoyable work environments.

NIGEL ROWE

The Book Guild Ltd

First published in Great Britain in 2022 by
The Book Guild Ltd
Unit E2 Airfield Business Park,
Harrison Road, Market Harborough,
Leicestershire. LE16 7UL
Tel: 0116 2792299
www.bookguild.co.uk
Email: info@bookguild.co.uk
Twitter: @bookguild

Typeset in 11pt Minion Pro

Printed and bound by CPI Group (UK) Ltd, Croydon, CR0 4YY

ISBN 978 1914471 704

British Library Cataloguing in Publication Data.
A catalogue record for this book is available from the British Library.

This book is dedicated to Ron and Joy Rowe, my dad and mum.

The first leaders I knew and from whom I learnt so very much.

CONTENTS

INTRODUCTION

How many leaders have you worked for?

How many other people have you been led by?

How many leaders have influenced you?

I asked myself these questions and surprised myself when I thought deeply about the impact of leadership on my life as well as my own role as a leader.

I have worked for over thirty-five years in the telecoms and media industries, renowned for being fast-moving and ever-changing. I've had roles ranging from being a graduate software engineer to being a board director and reporting to the CEO. But I've always had a boss.

I have worked for about thirty different bosses in my career so far. Plus, there have also been thirty bosses' bosses who have led the wider teams that I have been part of. And then other leaders who have indirectly led me when I have been on assignment for specific projects. Plus, peer groups of leaders and wider leadership teams and initiatives that I have been part of. Also, customers who I have done work for, delivering services and taking direction from the leadership of their organisations. And suppliers and partners where I have worked closely with the leaders.

And that's just in the workplace, specifically in my career since graduating from university.

Like most people, the first leaders I had were my parents, who were a massive influence. Then there were teachers at school, leaders of the clubs and societies I joined, cub scouts, youth clubs, the swimming club. Then there were my first part-time jobs when I was at school which ranged from working in a fish and chip shop to wiping down tables in a motorway service station, each with a variety of managers and leadership styles.

Over the course of our lives, we all experience being led by a wide range of leaders, some average, some poor, some terrible, some great and some brilliant and truly inspirational.

When I reflect on all the leaders that I have worked for and with, without a doubt, more than anything else, they have influenced:

- What it felt like to be in that role or part of that organisation.
- How much I enjoyed the role – my job satisfaction.
- My opportunity for personal growth, development and challenge.
- Whether I wanted to stay in the organisation.

Right from the start, I came to realise that there were two extremes of leaders. People who were fantastic to work for, who were inspiring, who motivated me and made work enjoyable and fun. Leaders that I wanted to follow and be like. Then there were the leaders who were the exact opposite, often creating a fear or blame culture, poor direction and team spirit and jobs that were anything but fun.

Of course, usually leaders would fit somewhere between these two extremes, with a mix of characteristics.

As a leader myself, I have learned many lessons. Often through mistakes and bitter experience at various times as I have tried hard to develop my leadership skills and be my best self.

Over the course of my career, I have learned from every leader I have worked for or interacted with, through both positive and negative experiences.

I have experienced leadership in a wide range of situations. In exciting periods of rapid growth and expansion. In times of crisis – I have worked for a company where a site caught fire and another that survived going through bankruptcy. Different circumstances which bring their own challenges and so often drive people to their extremes, either their very best or their very worst. Indeed, it is at the most difficult and stressful times that our true characters and deep attributes appear most clearly.

As I have endeavoured to become a better leader and learned from those around me as well as my own personal development, there are some key leadership qualities and ways of working that I have come to value highly.

These are the ones that I am truly passionate about. Those which I believe really make the difference between an average leader and a brilliant leader.

They reflect two main attributes – being positive and having a passion for people.

Positivity is all about being upbeat, creating clarity, providing direction and purpose, creating freshness, fun and warmth. Showing true professionalism and respect for others.

Having a passion for people is about putting people first. A leadership style which is all about caring and showing humanity. Striving to develop everyone to their full potential, inside or outside of the organisation. Being open and transparent and always acting with integrity, especially when implementing decisions which impact people. Valuing other people, their wellness and the need for a healthy work-life balance.

This is a leadership style which I call *Positive People Leadership*.

In today's world most people will be working for longer than previous generations, due to higher life expectancy and later retirement dates. With a long-term mortgage and more commitments outside of work to balance. There is a real shift towards healthier lifestyles and having a decent work-life balance. People, quite rightly, will no longer put up with old-school cultures of autocratic task-focused leaders who burn everyone out with long working hours in highly political, inefficient environments. In my view, these cultures are doomed and everyone with choice will want work to be a much better life experience.

Positive People Leaders are passionate about new world values, making their organisations the ones that everyone wants to be part of. Creating success by building highly motivated teams who love coming to work and achieve amazing things together.

In this book, I have put together fifty short summaries

of the factors which I believe sum up Positive People Leadership, grouped into the following five themes:

- Fundamentals
- Your leadership style
- Leading your team
- Your stakeholders – peers, partners and customers
- Techniques and tips

Each of the fifty descriptions are deliberately short (some very short). They are designed to be quickly digestible and to make you think.

Together they will enable you to drive positive culture change. To create fulfilling, rewarding and enjoyable environments for you and your teams. And through this, drive successful outcomes for your people, your organisation and yourself.

You can read the whole book very quickly from cover to cover if you wish, or you could choose to read one item a week as a 'thought for the week'. Then reflect on how to apply it in your own style of leadership if it resonates with you.

Don't be afraid to experiment and try things out. Above all, spend time reflecting, getting feedback from others around you, particularly the people you serve as a leader, and learning, adapting and growing. And let your positivity and passion shine through!

FUNDAMENTALS

The first section of this book covers the fundamental aspects of Positive People Leadership. Ten items which for me sum up what this is all about:

- Be passionate about people
- Have a clear vision
- Be positive
- Be true to yourself and act with integrity
- Be approachable
- Be customer-focused
- Live your company's cultural values
- Be human
- Create work-life balance
- Make work enjoyable

If you are a leader, you lead people, directly or indirectly. You deliver results through people. Whilst you may provide direction and make key decisions, ultimately whether you succeed or fail will be through the hard work of other people. Positive People Leaders are passionate about people. Passionate about creating environments and cultures where people are inspired to achieve their best and, above all, feel cared for.

If you are passionate about people, they will value working for you. Many years later, they will remember what it felt like working for you, more than what you achieved or the tasks that were performed. This is what makes the difference and is what your true reputation as a leader will be built on throughout your career.

Many people are naturally positive, but for some of us it takes a major life event to make us truly put things into perspective. I fell into that category. About ten years ago, I was out jogging one sunny morning, feeling fit and healthy, when I suddenly felt a sharp chest pain. It turned out that completely out of the blue, I was having a heart attack. Fortunately, I was rushed to hospital and the prompt action taken by excellent paramedics and a surgeon almost certainly saved my life. It took me several weeks to regain fitness, and during that time, I had a chance to reflect on my life, and in doing so, gain a fresh perspective. My overwhelming feeling was of being immensely grateful to be alive and determined to make the most out of every day. Overall, this experience has given me a substantially more positive attitude to my life. It also helped me to realise how important it is to enjoy every aspect of work and life and not get stressed by insignificant things.

Before this time, my work-life balance was fairly poor. At one point in particular in my career, just after a promotion, I found myself struggling to keep up with the demands of my new role and slipped into the habit of reopening my laptop in the evenings after I had arrived home from work and often at weekends to 'clear the backlog'. This habit went on for years until I received some valuable feedback from one of my team members, when I finally paused and considered what I was doing. Working extra hours when I was tired just meant that my efficiency dropped, and I wasn't actually very productive. The emails that I was sending to my team and colleagues put pressure on them, setting the wrong expectations and driving a poor work-life balance culture for everyone else as well as me. And my family was suffering, as my work time was eating into time I should have been spending with them. I am now much more respectful of other people's time – this is now a core value for me and an essential part of Positive People Leadership.

BE PASSIONATE
ABOUT PEOPLE

The most fundamental attribute of a Positive People Leader is how they make people feel.

Whilst people can achieve (usually short-term) targets and goals by being ruthless, aggressive, task-focused and rude, this is not a great way to lasting achievement.

Positive People Leaders take people with them. They judge success not just by achieving a target but by how they go about it. They achieve shared goals with their teams, acknowledge the contribution of others and because they empower and make the people that work with them feel great, the whole team grows. So, the leader can move on to further success, with a strong team around them ready to grow into their role.

Be passionate about people by caring, developing, empowering and seeking to bring out the best in people. Help people to grow by providing feedback, coaching and support. This also means having the courage to have difficult conversations quickly when required to resolve issues, manage performance and provide guidance.

Being passionate about people isn't just a leadership style. It's a way of being. It needs to be part of your DNA and show in everything you say and do as a leader. How you make people feel. And what everyone feels about you.

Be passionate for people, and let it show in everything you do.

HAVE A CLEAR VISION

Being a Positive People Leader is about creating certainty and clarity on where the team is heading. Setting direction.

A great leader sets a clear vision for the teams that they lead that everyone can get behind. So that everyone knows where they are going and can get excited about the journey. They can align with it and become a united team with a common purpose.

A brilliant vision should have the following attributes:

- Describe the overall outcome the leader is seeking for the team
- Be inspirational and motivating
- Be extremely clear and simple
- Incorporate the leader's values

Set a clear vision and let everyone know what you stand for.

BE POSITIVE

Positive People Leaders look for the best in everything and everyone. You can see it in their body language and their behaviours. They smile a lot. They enjoy what they do.

Positive People Leaders thrive on challenges. They see problems as opportunities. They radiate a 'can-do' attitude. They lift the mood and light up the room with warmth and energy. Everyone wants to be led by a positive person. Positive leaders quickly create positive teams.

Be positive. It is infectious.

BE TRUE TO YOURSELF AND ACT WITH INTEGRITY

Whatever you have to do as a leader, always stay true to your personal values. After all, this is what you stand for.

Always act with integrity in everything that you do. We all have to do tough things as leaders. Make hard decisions. Have very difficult conversations. Impact people's lives. But in everything we do, in every action we take, we must never lose our integrity. Always act with honesty. With decency. Respectfully. Impartially. Be truthful at all times. And stand by any other personal values you have. They are what you are, and no one can force you to act out of line with them.

Be true to yourself and act with integrity. Always.

BE APPROACHABLE

Never be a person who people are afraid to give bad news to. The reality is that bad news is always around, some worse than others.

If you create an environment where people in your team are afraid to tell you about problems for fear of the consequences, the bad news will simply get buried. You won't hear about it. You will kid yourself that everything is fine when, in reality, problems are festering and growing around you.

You will then only get to hear about a problem when it has grown so big that people are absolutely forced to tell you about it or, worse still, something awful happens. By this time, the problem will be extremely bad, and you will have lost the opportunity to help and support your team and address it whilst it was small and fixable.

There are examples in all industries of disasters which could have been avoided if only the leaders had known about the problems earlier.

Positive People Leaders are always approachable. They know what is going on and can support their teams because everyone can be fully open and transparent with them.

BE CUSTOMER-FOCUSED

Be customer-focused in all that you do.

Positive People Leaders know and understand their customers, both internal and external. Every stakeholder that they deliver a service to – directly or indirectly – is a customer. They make sure everyone in their team knows and understands this and that it becomes part of the DNA of the team.

Make sure you build teams that understand:

- Who your customers are
- What customers need from the team
- How to deliver a brilliant service – as judged by the customer
- That customers are the fundamental reason that the team exists

Regularly measure how your customers feel about you and your team, about what you deliver and how you deliver it. Share feedback with your teams and together take ownership for your customer service improvement journey. Think of interesting and imaginative ways to invite your customers into your team and have great interactions. Make your customers want to do business with you. More than anyone else.

LIVE YOUR COMPANY'S
CULTURAL VALUES

Buy into the cultural values of your organisation. Totally. If you are lucky enough to be in a newly formed or transformed business where values are being born, contribute to the set-up of them. When you join a new company, make sure you fully understand their values. Make this a key part of your decision-making as to whether you join or not.

Live your company's values in everything that you do. Bring them to life in your behaviours and actions. Great values are the lifeblood of a great company. If you can't buy into your company's values in this way, then it is the wrong company for you. If this is the case, get out – quickly.

BE HUMAN

As a leader, you will often have to do hard things. Have difficult conversations. Give constructive feedback. Communicate bad news. Deal with poor performance. Make people redundant.

Never shirk or procrastinate on these important responsibilities. Do these hard things as soon as they need to be done and act professionally. But above all, show humanity in the way you do them.

Positive People Leaders always treat people with respect in all their interactions, especially the difficult ones.

Be strong. Be solid and purposeful. But also be human and show the other person that you care about them. They might not like the message that you have to deliver to them. You can't change that. But you are responsible for how you give it and the way that you act.

Be human. Always treat people with respect. They will remember *how* you managed the interaction, even if it was a really hard thing you had to do.

CREATE WORK-LIFE BALANCE

There are some cultures where working exceptionally long hours is expected. Where people are phoned up for trivial things out of hours or at weekends. Where everyone feels obliged to check their emails when they are on holiday.

This is not a sign of a great team or of motivated performers. It's a big red warning light that something is very wrong with the organisation. Working this way is incredibly inefficient, and it burns people out.

When it comes to a decent work-life balance, Positive People Leaders set the standard by their actions. This is a classic area where leading by example is everything.

Positive People Leaders recognise that everyone needs to have a healthy balance. To recharge and refresh. To live a fulfilling life outside of work with family, friends and leisure activities. They respect other people's personal time and expect this in return.

It's a well-known fact that people with a balanced life outside of work perform far more effectively and are more productive. As well as being happier, healthier and motivated.

Of course, we all need to put in extra hours and make sacrifices from time to time. Most people would accept that. But be careful not to encourage and reward poor work-life balance behaviours. Always hold your meetings during normal working hours and encourage people to take regular breaks.

Working from home can help by reducing travel and providing flexibility, but it can also be a nightmare for managing a separation between work and home life. Be very aware of this and encourage your team to switch off fully at the times when they are not working.

Be sure to create a strong work-life balance culture in your team. It will increase motivation and productivity as well as driving trust and effective delegation when people are on holiday.

MAKE WORK ENJOYABLE

No one wants to spend the majority of their life doing something they don't enjoy. But it's amazing how many people do not like the jobs that they do. Who live for the weekend and start to feel a sinking feeling every Sunday evening. It just doesn't need to be like that.

Positive People Leaders strive to make work enjoyable. This doesn't mean that it's not hard work. Or without challenges and the inevitable highs and lows.

There are two things that Positive People Leaders do:
1) Set up an environment where work is fun
2) Make sure people are in the right roles

Setting up the right environment is key and there are many ideas in this book. It's also about keeping a healthy level of challenge for everyone, whilst calling out and removing unnecessary sources of stress. Looking at each aspect of the role and how to increase satisfaction from it. Not taking things too seriously and finding time to have fun.

Leaders have to make hard judgement calls to make sure each person is in the right role. All too often, people find themselves trapped in a role that is just wrong for them. This is bad for them, the rest of the team and for the company. The Positive People Leader's role is to help to resolve this.

SUMMARY: FUNDAMENTALS

- Being passionate about people is the underlying principle of Positive People Leadership. Genuinely caring about the people you lead, work with and serve and letting it show in everything you do and the way that you do it. Thinking about the people aspects of every decision that you make.
- Setting a clear vision means providing direction and purpose, but it is also about simplicity. Making what you stand for easy to understand, relate to and remember.
- You know a positive person from the very first instant you see them. They literally brighten up the room and glow with optimism and energy.
- Acting with integrity is something we all strive to do, but staying absolutely true to this when times are tough is an essential attribute of a Positive People Leader.
- Being approachable sounds obvious, but poor or inexperienced leaders often react terribly when they are presented with bad news. This quickly creates an environment where people no longer open up to them and bury problems, only for them to fester and grow.

- Viewing all of the people that you provide a service to as your customer, and striving to give them the best, can make a profound difference. It's incredible how people in many organisations still fail to understand this basic concept and treat others as a nuisance, rather than the reason that their job exists.
- Make sure you fully understand the cultural values of your organisation before you join it. Talk to people who work there and form a view whether the values are a statement of intent or the lifeblood of the business. This should be a critical factor in your decision whether you want to work there.
- All leaders have to do tough things, some of which can have a major impact on the people they lead. Positive People Leaders care deeply about *how* they implement hard decisions. They always act with humanity and treat people respectfully in all situations.
- Creating work-life balance has never been more important, and it is essential to lead by example. Positive People Leaders always make sure that everyone is getting a decent chance to fully refresh themselves. Not just their teams, of course, but everyone that they influence or assign work to.
- We often talk about work being challenging. A challenge can be something we enjoy and gain satisfaction and pride from doing. Or it can be something that causes great stress. All too often this is about leadership and culture. Finding ways to make challenges feel enjoyable and people feel great is what Positive People Leaders do naturally.

YOUR LEADERSHIP STYLE

This section explores leadership style, with ten things which I would advise you to do as a Positive People Leader. These are characteristics which will make you stand out and make a positive difference to both the people that you lead and yourself. They are:

- Thank people, always
- Ask stupid questions
- Control your voice
- Enable people to perform at their best
- Welcome feedback
- Allow people to learn from their mistakes
- When times are tough, make people feel like heroes… not zeros
- Acknowledge the contribution of others
- Be a mentor
- Actively manage performance

I always feel a warm glow when someone says thank you to me – we all like to be appreciated. I remember one time when I had to do a presentation to the company leadership team of about fifty people, including all of the board members. I had prepared intensely for it and was fairly nervous, but it went well. The next day, I received a thank-you note from the CEO, saying how useful he had found the presentation.

I have never forgotten that he took the time to do this and how proud it made me feel.

Many years ago, I worked for a small company which ran a national mobile radio network providing communications for lorries, buses and county councils. One Friday, pretty much out of the blue, we had a crisis. One of the three specialised computer systems that managed all of the calls in London and the south-east of England went into overload and started to fail, putting the whole business at risk. Angry customers were calling in and urgent action had to be taken. Myself and my team had to deal with the emergency by working with our supplier to replace a critical part of the system that weekend, something that would normally take months. It was very stressful, but we dealt with it, and by Monday morning we had succeeded and could then take stock and begin to work out why it had happened without any of us seeing it coming.

What I remember most from this experience though was how the leaders above me behaved, particularly on the Friday night. They kept calm, despite the intense pressure, and were supportive. They made me and my team feel like heroes who were saving the company. They could so easily have shown frustration and anger and looked for someone to blame, which would have demotivated and distracted us all. Instead, we were supported all the way. And learned some valuable lessons.

In these situations, Positive People Leadership is everything.

THANK PEOPLE, ALWAYS

Always make time to say thank you. Say thank you by email or write a note so that the person can look at it again, save it, share it and show it to their family if they wish.

But also say thank you in person as well. Get out there and shake someone's hand as you let them know you appreciate what they have done for you. Be sincere at all times. Let them see your gratitude in your face and body language. Go and find them so they know you have made the time and effort to seek them out to say thanks. Call out achievements publicly. And individually. Make people who have done great things feel great.

ASK STUPID QUESTIONS

Never be worried about asking a stupid question. If you don't understand something, always ask for clarification. Watch the relief around the room when you ask your question; you are rarely the only one who doesn't understand. There will be others who also didn't get it but were afraid to admit it. After all, it's how we learn.

Let everyone know that you like to make sure you understand and have clarity. They will respect you for it. You are also demonstrating that you are fully engaged in what the other person is trying to communicate to you. And you will be amazed how often what appears to be a stupid question is actually quite perceptive and creates better insight for everyone.

Be the one who asks the stupid questions and encourage this in others.

CONTROL YOUR VOICE

Control your voice; think about how it sounds to others in different situations.

Speak with passion, energy and enthusiasm. Use pitch and pauses as well as words to convey what you mean in a way that shows you are speaking from your heart.

Always speak with sincerity. Listen to yourself. Know how you come across to others. And however frustrated you may get, never ever shout. You can be a strong leader without having to overly raise your voice. No one likes shouty people.

ENABLE PEOPLE TO
PERFORM AT THEIR BEST

Positive People Leaders take responsibility to enable people to develop and grow to achieve their full potential. They look for and see the best in them and nurture it. They understand that they themselves don't directly produce results; they deliver through people. These people need to be engaged and perform at their best for the team to be successful.

Grow people for better things. Help them to find their best self. When the time is right, help them move on, either within the company or outside of the company if there is no suitable position. Never hold people back or stifle their growth. Help them to their next opportunity willingly. Set them free. Rejoice when they move on to bigger things.

Positive People Leaders enable people to perform at their best.

WELCOME FEEDBACK

Good, honest feedback is invaluable. If you are serious about developing yourself then it's a vital input that you need from everyone around you: your team, your boss, your peers, your customers. Also, from your friends and family. Ask others for feedback. Regularly.

But asking for feedback is not enough. You can tell others that you welcome feedback – that also is not enough. To be really open to feedback you have to demonstrate it firstly by the way that you receive it. And then by what you do with it.

Sincerely thank the person for their feedback. Whether you like it or not, their opinion is a really important insight for you, and they have invested their time, thought and effort in providing it. Of course, it's entirely your decision to assess the inputs and decide whether and how to act on the feedback you receive. For each piece of feedback that you decide to act on, be sure to share the results and outcome back to the person who gave you feedback.

Welcome feedback and create a powerful and rewarding development cycle for yourself. Lead by example and encourage this in others too.

ALLOW PEOPLE TO LEARN
FROM THEIR MISTAKES

Organisations sometimes describe themselves as having a learning culture, but often they don't really mean it. Their leaders are too afraid that a person who has made a mistake and learnt from it will make the mistake again. So, they hire someone else without experience who then makes the same mistake. The first person had real wisdom.

Sadly, people who have learnt the most often don't stay with their organisations. They seem to lose the trust of their leaders, who don't realise the value that has been created. So, these people take their hard-earned experience to other companies, where they do incredible things.

How much better would it be if they had stayed and applied their learnings? To use their insight to make a difference, rather than letting someone else make the same mistakes.

Positive People Leaders trust people who demonstrate that they can learn from their mistakes. They know that these people have the potential to apply their learnings to become amazing.

WHEN TIMES ARE TOUGH, MAKE PEOPLE FEEL LIKE HEROES... NOT ZEROS

Sometimes things are tough and you're running from behind. Something has gone wrong. You're off plan. Or you're losing a bid. Or market share is down. Or you're three-nil down at half time.

And your role as a Positive People Leader is to turn it round. That's the time to make your team feel like heroes. Think how you want them to feel. Like heroes with the challenge of seizing the opportunity to do something incredible. To save the day. To make things right for the organisation. To achieve something that is truly career enhancing for them.

The alternative approach that so many poor leaders take is to make their team feel terrible that they are in this mess. To make them feel worthless and blamed. To feel the full force of their anger and frustration rather than support and encouragement.

Same situation... two possible approaches.

Positive People Leaders motivate people. They inspire their teams to see the opportunity to make a difference. To rise to the challenge. To feel like heroes. And to celebrate the successes that follow, every step of the way.

ACKNOWLEDGE THE
CONTRIBUTION OF OTHERS

The results we achieve are rarely just the product of individual effort. Most of what we do is delivered with the help and support of others around us.

Make sure that when you are the one presenting a report, delivering the results or accepting praise for a successful outcome, you acknowledge everyone who has helped to create it.

Positive People Leaders deliver by bringing together the combined efforts of others. With many other stakeholders inside and outside an organisation. With help from their peers, their bosses, their mentors. And most of all from their teams.

Clearly call out others who have supported you and show your appreciation. Let the team take the credit for a great team outcome.

Always take the opportunity and make the time to acknowledge the contribution of everyone who has helped you.

BE A MENTOR

Mentoring comes naturally to Positive People Leaders. It's a key part of their make-up to want to develop others.

Put the offer out there to be a mentor. Inside and outside your team. Inside and outside your company. In fact, not even just within your industry sector.

Expect people that you mentor to respect your time and use it wisely to get value. Ask them to be clear what they are seeking out of you as a mentor and to prepare for each session. In turn, your role as a mentor is to listen, support, feed back and challenge. To use your experience to guide and offer suggestions, help and encouragement.

There is huge value and reward in the experience for you too. It's a two-way process; we all learn from each other continually. You will build great relationships which can last for years. And be sure to get yourself a mentor too.

ACTIVELY MANAGE
PERFORMANCE

As a Positive People Leader, your role is to manage poor performance. This is actually an extension of the principle of bringing out the best in everyone you lead.

Be sure to tackle poor performance. Quickly. Take action to address it fast. Work with the person to understand the reasons and seek solutions. Especially when there is a difficult conversation to be held or a hard decision to make about someone's role.

Also, make sure that performance is managed well throughout your teams. Poor behaviours should never be tolerated. Someone who behaves badly with a poor attitude, and who is unwilling to change, should have no place in the organisation, and the leader's role is to exit them quickly.

Someone with a good attitude and behaviours who is underperforming is a development opportunity. Here, the leader's role is to call out the issue, understand the reasons and help to turn the situation round.

SUMMARY: YOUR LEADERSHIP STYLE

- It takes very little time to say thank you, to show people that you appreciate their contribution. Do it often, sincerely and personally.
- Ask stupid questions (which will often turn out to be not so stupid). Lead by example and never hold back for fear of looking less knowledgeable.
- The tone of your voice, and the body language that accompanies it, will set an instant impression on those around you. When times get challenging, it will reveal who you really are.
- Enabling people to perform at their best is the lifelong mission of a Positive People Leader. Helping people to grow and develop is one of the most rewarding things you can do. Sometimes this can be tough if you have to actively move someone who is in the wrong role or have courageous conversations to manage poor performance.

- Positive People Leaders always give and encourage feedback. Remember that you have to demonstrate that you are really open to feedback by the way in which you receive it. It is your decision on whether and how to use it.
- Take some personal risk to give people the room to learn from their mistakes and continue to fully stand behind them. Create a true learning culture.
- When times get tough, show support and encouragement, rather than anger and frustration. It's the time to make people feel valued and inspired to turn the situation round. To create something incredible and memorable.
- Always acknowledge the contribution that others have made. It's never just the work of one person and there will always be people, often behind the scenes, without whom there would not have been a successful outcome.
- Offer to be a mentor to others. Use your experience to guide and help people develop. Mentor people who actively seek your help and expect them to respect your time and use it wisely.
- Actively manage poor performance. Never tolerate poor behaviours, but approach someone with a good attitude and behaviours as a development opportunity.

LEADING
YOUR TEAM

In this section I have listed ten things which specifically relate to leading your team. They may seem obvious, but when you read through each page, challenge yourself as to whether you really do these.

- Serve your team
- Give people space and flexibility when they need it
- Be calm in a crisis
- Show up at social events
- Give your team visibility
- Invite your boss in
- Build your team with different people
- Hold regular team updates
- Hold off-site team charity days
- Invest in learning and development

A company I once worked for had about three hundred people based at our local factory site. Just enough space to hold the annual Christmas lunch in the on-site restaurant in two sittings. For this very memorable occasion, the managing director decided to hold a medieval banquet-style event. The tables were laid out in rows, there was lively music and plenty of food and drink for everyone.

What made this different was that the MD and the members of his board served the food. Myself and all of the other hundreds of employees sat on our tables and the senior management team waited on us. They spent the entire time moving amongst the tables, cheerfully serving out food and drink and making merry conversation with everyone. They were even dressed up in medieval costumes for extra effect.

A very simple but effective idea which, in a fun way, made a big statement – as leaders they were there to serve their teams. Of course, their wider actions also reflected this same approach, otherwise this would have been meaningless. It was a great company to work for.

If you have never arranged or taken part in a team charity day, then I would strongly encourage you to try it out. I have done this on a number of occasions, ranging from painting the fences at a local school to helping create gardens at a hospice. Each time, arranged by a member of the team, was a memorable team-building day which brought everyone together doing something really worthwhile.

SERVE YOUR TEAM

Always remember that Positive People Leadership is about serving people, whether you are the leader of a small team, a CEO or the president/prime minister of your country.

As a leader, you are accountable for the performance of your team. Serve the team by making sure they have clarity and direction. Serve the team by understanding what they need to succeed. By creating the right environment for them to function brilliantly. By unblocking issues and obstacles. And, of course, celebrating successes and key achievements.

But also by cheering everyone on during challenging times. By being supportive when things don't go so well and taking accountability. Helping to understand key learnings and lift the spirit when necessary. To be better next time and continuously improve.

Positive People Leaders serve their people. Make sure you provide a brilliant service to your team.

GIVE PEOPLE SPACE AND
FLEXIBILITY WHEN THEY NEED IT

We all have difficult times in our lives, some sadly have more than their fair share. Health issues, bereavements, family members who fall ill, emergencies of all kinds.

When someone in your team has a problem that they need to deal with, give them the space and flexibility that they need. Straight away. Make sure that at a time of personal difficulty, work is not something they need to worry about. Reassure them that you will take care of things. Offer support if it's needed. But, above all, make sure that you take responsibility for putting arrangements in place to cover the work and let others know as appropriate. Then, as things get better, if they need flexibility in their return to work, provide it.

Give people space and flexibility when they most need it. They will remember how you acted and respect you for it. And there really is no other way to act if you are a Positive People Leader.

BE CALM IN A CRISIS

Being able to stay calm in a crisis or when there is a major problem is a sign of true leadership. It's the time when you need to think clearly. Most importantly, it's also the time when your experts who can fix the problem need to think clearly. And perform at their best.

Positive People Leaders quickly understand the problem and take action to make sure the right experts are assigned – usually not themselves (as leaders may not be the experts). And then they give them the space they need.

They stay updated but don't interfere in the detail. They provide guidance and direction when they need to. They support the team with everything they need, from supplier escalations and extra resources to sorting hotels and supplies of coffee and pizza.

The leader keeps everyone else fully informed about the issue – what the problem is, what the impact is and the steps being taken – until it is resolved. So that the expert team is not distracted.

Good leaders and organisations will have incident plans which click into place at these times – to ensure that the experts are known and available, the stakeholders and their roles are defined throughout the organisation, accountabilities are clear and there is a well-managed communications plan.

SHOW UP AT SOCIAL EVENTS

Always make the effort to get to work-related social events – Christmas parties, team dinners, charity fundraisers and the like. Showing up says that you care. It's your opportunity to get to know your team better and for them to get to know you. You don't have to stay right to the end of a lively Christmas party; it's sometimes best to give the team some space…

But leaders that always show up and support are valued by their teams.

GIVE YOUR TEAM VISIBILITY

Promote your team to the rest of your business. Make sure everyone in your organisation knows who the team is and what value they bring to the organisation.

Create a brand for your team. Work with your team to put together your story: your purpose, why you exist, what everyone does, your past achievements and your future goals and targets. Then take your story out to the rest of the business with members of your team. Know your audiences and make it interesting and exciting to each of them.

Remember, as a Positive People Leader, you are also the Marketing Director for your team.

INVITE YOUR BOSS IN

Invite your boss to your meetings from time to time. Make sure you give her/him a chance to meet and engage with your team. Use these occasions to give your team more visibility. Get your team to share their achievements. Also, use these as opportunities for really open Q&A sessions. If you are uncomfortable with doing this, think hard and understand why. The problem is either you or your boss. If you have built a wall around your team, break it down. If you are embarrassed to put your boss in front of your team, you are working for the wrong boss – you need to find a new one.

BUILD YOUR TEAM WITH
DIFFERENT PEOPLE

Make sure your team shares the same values and purpose and exhibits great behaviours – this is absolutely fundamental. But beyond this, seek diversity. Build your team with different people, who can each bring a variety of opinions and interesting experiences to the group. If everyone thinks the same way as you, as a team you will be restricted and narrow in your thinking. Teams built in the image of their leader can suffer from this badly. Diverse teams challenge the leader and each other. They have rich discussions. They are creative.

They can also be difficult to lead, particularly whilst they are still forming. Your role as a Positive People Leader is to make the most of everyone in the team. To create an orchestra rather than just a string section. To create a football team rather than a group of centre forwards.

Build your team from different people. The best teams are united in their values, purpose and behaviours but have great variety and can be built from an unlikely combination of characters. They take a little more time to evolve but then become incredibly effective.

HOLD REGULAR TEAM UPDATES

Get your whole team together. Regularly. Give them an update on what's happening. Whatever you have. Even if there is not much to say. Keep it regular.

Be open and transparent. Vary the format. Use different venues and locations. Make it interesting.

Use these sessions to do all of these things:

- Share news
- Give visibility to people in the team
- Celebrate successes – buy cakes!
- Introduce new people
- Invite others from different teams in
- Answer questions on any topic

Get others in the team to participate and give updates. Ask your team to help to set the agenda. Choose a time that works well for everyone. And make time afterwards to socialise.

HOLD OFF-SITE
TEAM CHARITY DAYS

Look for opportunities to get your team together outside of the office. To do something different together. All too often, off-site team days are spent in a dark and dreary hotel room, suffocating under reams of heavy PowerPoint decks. Information sharing, maybe. But not team building.

Your team-building days can and should be so much more than just a day out of the office together. They should be opportunities to enjoy each other's company in different surroundings. To build the team by working on a non-work project together that is a new experience. To do something really worthwhile.

Providing help to a charity for a day is a perfect way to do this. There are loads of charities that look for this type of help.

Ask the team for suggestions. Organise the day yourself or, better still, ask for a team member to volunteer to project manage it.

Have a brilliant off-site day doing something incredibly

worthwhile that you and your team can be proud of. You will be amazed how much better it is than stuffy PowerPoint and also at how great this type of event is at really building your team.

INVEST IN LEARNING
AND DEVELOPMENT

Create a culture of continuous improvement in your team. Where everyone is encouraged to both take and make opportunities to develop and learn.

We learn from everything we do. Often, the most powerful lessons are from those things that didn't go well, so especially make sure that your team understand that these learnings are acknowledged and valued by you.

Be sure to hold reviews at the end of every major activity or project. Use these to discuss what went well. What didn't go well. What the key learnings were. And produce an action plan to build on successes and make changes to improve.

Also, make sure everyone in the team has a development plan. Which they take ownership for, with you or their line manager as the enabler. It's a two-way thing.

Learning and development needs to be active, engaging, living, breathing. Don't just talk about sending people on training courses – try the following:

- Hold talent reviews with your peers, make rising stars visible
- Seek secondment opportunities to broaden the experience of team members
- Run knowledge-sharing sessions; encourage sharing of expertise and learnings

And of course, do provide lots of formal training and send people to conferences. Ask those attending to be clear on what development outcome they are seeking. Then request that they agree to play back what they learnt to the team afterwards as a knowledge share. This will help everyone but also provide focus for those attending on what specific benefits that have gained.

SUMMARY: LEADING

YOUR TEAM

- Leadership is about serving people. Make sure you are providing a brilliant service to your team. Always.
- We all have moments in our life when we need flexibility. Positive People Leaders recognise these times and take prompt action to provide support and give people space to deal with the situation, without having to worry about work.
- Stay calm in times of crisis and create an environment where everyone can think clearly and perform at their best, without unnecessary distraction. At these times, cool, calm leadership is essential.
- Attending work-related social events shows your support and that you care. It's also a great way to really get to know your team.
- Work with your team to put together your story. Then take it out and present it with them to the rest of your organisation and your partners – make everyone aware

of the team and the value that they add.

- Invite your boss into your team meetings from time to time and let your team share their achievements with them.
- Seek to build diverse teams with a broad combination of skills, strengths, opinions and experience, united by the same values and great behaviours. With the ability to challenge you and each other to explore solutions and deliver the best outcomes.
- Hold team updates regularly, built on openness and transparency. Vary the format to make them interesting and encourage others in the team to take part.
- Hold team-building days that really build (rather than bore) the team. Do something worthwhile for charity together.
- Make learning and development active and engaging in all aspects of the team's activities. Hold lessons learned reviews to share experiences openly, and make sure that everyone in the team has a personal development plan which they take ownership for.

YOUR STAKEHOLDERS – PEERS/ PARTNERS/ CUSTOMERS

In this section, I have grouped together ten items that relate to your interactions with others:

- Make everyone a great ambassador for the team
- Know your customers and serve them well
- Buddy up and knowledge share
- Set up win-win partnerships
- Be the best customer
- Visit your partners
- Be welcoming to others
- Develop and grow your network
- Pick the right boss
- Be a role model to your wider team

Everyone talks about being customer-focused or customer-centric, but it is incredible how many people don't actually understand who all of their customers are. All too often, I encounter situations where people act like their customers are an inconvenience, a nuisance or simply that they are doing them a favour.

And regardless how great you are at presenting yourself to your customers, partners and others, your team is a key part of your brand. If just one person in your team presents an unfriendly or discourteous impression in any of their actions, then that shapes the image of everyone.

Contrast that with a team full of warm, friendly, positive and enthusiastic people, to whom nothing is a problem – real ambassadors for your team who are ready to help and serve. This is the team that Positive People Leaders delight in creating.

The best organisations and leaders apply positive principles to partnerships with their suppliers, recognising that lasting success is about sustainable win-win arrangements which benefit both organisations. I have seen too many situations over the years where decisions were made on lowest bid price only, from suppliers who overcommitted to get the business from overdemanding customers. And in doing so, setting up a future world of poor delivery performance and a terrible working relationship before the contract was even signed. It just doesn't need to be like that.

The buddy up and knowledge share idea is built from a time when I worked closely with a finance team, and we quickly realised that my team of engineers knew very little about finance and similarly, the finance team didn't understand how a mobile phone network worked. So, we put them in a room together with a whiteboard for two sessions. One for the engineers to explain in super simple terms how the phone network worked and the second session for the finance team to explain everything an engineer needed to know about basic company finance and management accounting. Informal 'ask anything you like' sessions, with coffee and cake helpfully provided. Knowledge share at its best, plus great relationship-building across different teams.

MAKE EVERYONE A GREAT AMBASSADOR FOR THE TEAM

The image of your team is set by everyone who is in it. By the way you all act. With all of your interactions with others.

You share in one brand. So, make sure everyone shares the same brand values. Anyone interfacing with your team will form an instant impression based on their first interaction with any team member. The person who calls your assistant to request a meeting with you. The customer who meets one of your team members on their site. Your peers who ask someone in the team for help – with anything.

Positive People Leaders build teams with enthusiastic, courteous, helpful people who see everyone as their customer. Who will willingly go the extra mile for anyone. Everyone is an ambassador and sets the image for the team. How do you want your team to be seen?

KNOW YOUR CUSTOMERS
AND SERVE THEM WELL

Your customers are anyone that you provide a service of any kind to. Inside or outside of the organisation. Any person at every level in any function that you deliver anything to.

Make sure you know who all of your customers are. Make sure you know what they want from you and how they expect it to be delivered. What good looks like for them. Then, with this understanding, set out to overachieve it. Big time.

As a Positive People Leader, your role is to ensure that the whole of your team provides not just a good or a great service but a brilliant service that you can all be proud of. Make this the attitude that exists throughout your team in all that you do and especially in the way that you do it. Make all of your customers feel special and delighted with the service you give them.

Make sure your customers know that you want to continually raise the bar. Demonstrate this by proactively seeking feedback from them. Share the feedback throughout the team. Celebrate great feedback when you get it. Call out those people in the team who demonstrate brilliant customer-orientated behaviours. And let the team take ownership for your continuous improvement plan.

BUDDY UP AND
KNOWLEDGE SHARE

Each team within a business is a mini centre of excellence. It has a part to play in the overall function of the organisation, with unique skills. And often a set of jargon and language that goes with it.

Buddying up with another team is a great way to broaden everyone's knowledge and build relationships. To increase understanding and appreciate what others do.

Set a session up where one team presents to the other what they do and what their specialist skills are. What their goals, priorities and outcomes are. What's important to them. Then have a free-flowing Q&A session. Or better still, a 'teach in' session to really share knowledge. Then hold the session again, the other way round.

This works with similar functions, and it also works with completely unrelated areas. Everyone has something to give and something to learn.

Work with other leaders in your business to set up knowledge-share sessions. You will be amazed at how effective they are.

SET UP WIN-WIN
PARTNERSHIPS

Great partnerships with your suppliers are essential to create long-term success. It's critical that they are set up well from the outset.

When selecting a new partner, a decent price, strong capability and ability to meet the requirement is a given. Everyone does this, but on its own, it's not enough.

In fact, pushing too hard for a cheap price at the expense of other factors can be a very false economy indeed and simply create a very contractual relationship with no flexibility and lots of frustration every time your requirement changes or becomes clearer (which it inevitably will).

Positive People Leaders understand that great partnerships need to be win-win. So that both customer and partner grow successfully together – not one at the expense of the other.

What is critical beyond price, capability and ability is the how. How both parties commit to build the relationship and work together, through the life of the contract, with the inevitable ups and downs.

A strong partnership that is working well has great behaviours from the outset, exemplified by the leaders of both organisations. They won't be identical, as companies have their own identities and culture, but there needs to be alignment on the following:

- A willingness to invest in the partnership – especially to make sure the programme is well resourced and sponsored from the outset in both organisations
- Trust, openness, transparency at all levels
- The ability to hold each other to account
- Give and take, a willing level of flexibility on both sides
- A desire to create win-win outcomes
- Lots of knowledge-sharing between teams
- Regular, honest, two-way feedback
- A culture of continuous improvement
- Joint celebration events

BE THE BEST CUSTOMER

When you start a partnership with a supplier, ask yourself: how would we make ourselves the best customer they have? The customer that they would proudly boast about to everyone. That they would want to write about on their website. To use your organisation as a reference to attract other customers. To showcase what they do for you. A great case study.

Have this conversation with your partner at the start of your journey together. Set this as a shared goal, as a measure of success. Challenge yourselves as to whether you are setting up the relationship in this way. Make sure both of you are super clear what you are signing up to – a well-defined scope of what is wanted and a strong vision of how you will work together. For the long-term.

At the other extreme are the relationships that seem all too common. Deals driven solely by (apparent) lowest cost, overcommitment by suppliers and disappointment, arguments, contractual disputes and penalty threats all the way. Lose – lose by any measure.

Build on solid foundations with great behaviours. Be the best customer for your partners.

VISIT YOUR PARTNERS

Get out and visit your partners and suppliers.

Don't demand that they always come to you as you are the customer. That's lazy and sends a message that you think you are more important.

Get out and see them in their environment, whether it's just down the road or the other side of the world.

Create the opportunity to meet all of their people who are delivering for you. Not just the managers but everyone who is part of the delivery team. Ask to see where the work happens. Get out to site; get onto the factory floor; get to the office where the teams work. Introduce yourself to everyone. Observe and listen. Explain the value that the partner brings to your business. Help everyone to understand how important their contribution is to your customers. And take the opportunity to say thank you to each and every one of them. Shake lots of hands. Win some hearts and minds and really get to understand your partners. You will be amazed at how much insight you gain and how it improves productivity and the reputation of you and your company.

Get out and visit your partners and suppliers. Regularly.

BE WELCOMING TO OTHERS

We have all at some time or other felt nervous when we had to present to another group of people. Whether at a company board meeting or to a customer. We know that feeling.

So, when you invite someone into your environment, to your team meeting or other session that you run, put yourself in their place and imagine how they might feel. Maybe nervous or apprehensive.

Set expectations beforehand with them as to what is expected at the meeting. Be clear on any preparation required both from them and from you and the rest of the team in order to ensure a successful outcome.

At the meeting, seek immediately to put them at their ease. Smile. Let them know you are pleased they are with you. Make sure they are introduced to everyone. Set a warm and friendly tone. Help to set the session up for success. Ensure that your team have done any preparation. Make sure they are equally welcoming too.

DEVELOP AND GROW
YOUR NETWORK

Building and maintaining a strong network of people both inside and outside of your industry is critical to your success and growth. It is worth investing time and effort in. Constantly. It's so easy to stop networking when life gets busy. But make the effort to stay in touch.

Invest in your network:

- To connect with everyone you want to stay in touch with
- To help and support others
- To keep in touch with your industry – to stay informed
- To raise your profile and open up new opportunities
- To learn and find inspiration
- To draw on support from others when you need it

Networking is a bit like gardening. Spend time on it. Grow relationships and draw inspiration from a wide range of people who add brightness and diversity. Have a network that you are proud of. And weed out negative people; they have no place in it.

Build and invest in your network at all times. Not just when you are job-hunting.

PICK THE RIGHT BOSS

Choose your boss carefully. Find someone who is a great leader, who inspires you. Someone who will challenge, develop and stretch you. And support you when you need support. Who will help and encourage you to grow. Someone you can learn much from. Someone who is also open to challenge from you. To give you opportunities to help you both succeed.

Having the right boss has a major impact on whether you enjoy your role and find it fulfilling. Having a poor boss is one of the biggest reasons that people quit their jobs.

Choose your boss carefully. If you find that you have chosen poorly, then find yourself another one.

BE A ROLE MODEL
TO YOUR WIDER TEAM

Being a Positive People Leader is not just about leading your own team.

As well as leading your team, you will probably be part of a team with your peer group. The management team that you are part of. Or maybe part of the company's board. And probably a member of one or more virtual teams within the business, such as a senior leadership team or other cross-functional groups. Plus, you will interact with people in other teams as part of your role.

In all of these situations, you have a leadership role to perform to the wider organisation. As a manager, a senior manager, a director. A leader. Set an example of Positive People Leadership to your peer group. Take the opportunity to create and engage in any activities to help your peers or to lead virtual teams to drive wider company initiatives. To broaden your experience and visibility. To develop yourself and grow your personal brand of leadership.

And always remember that you are a leader within your

industry. Not just within your organisation. Not just a leader of your team. Be a role model to others wherever you are. In all situations. Ask yourself – what is your contribution to the wider team?

SUMMARY: YOUR STAKEHOLDERS – PEERS/ PARTNERS/CUSTOMERS

- The image of your team is made up of everyone who is in it. You share in one brand, so make sure you build teams where everyone is a great ambassador.
- Your customers are everyone that you provide a service of any kind to. Positive People Leaders create teams where everyone knows their customers and wants them to feel special by providing a brilliant service to them.
- Buddy your team up with another team for an informal knowledge-share session. It's great development for the team and it will build relationships across the organisation.
- Seek to create long-term win-win partnerships with your suppliers. Focus on how you will work together to create value throughout the life of the contract and invest in the relationship with trust, openness and transparency from the outset.

- Strive to be the customer that your partners are proudest to work with. To be their best customer that everyone in the partner organisation values the most and enjoys working with.

- Get out and visit your partners often. Understand their environment, introduce yourself to everyone and take the opportunity to thank all of the people who are working hard for you.

- When other people join your meetings or sessions that you run, be sure to be welcoming and immediately set a warm and friendly tone.

- Invest in building and maintaining your network at all times, not just when seeking a new role. Build a network you are proud of, and weed out negative people.

- Having an inspiring boss who will challenge, inspire and support your growth is essential. Remember that you can always choose to move on and find a new boss.

- Being a Positive People Leader is not just about leading your own team. It's about being a role model within and outside of the organisation.

TECHNIQUES
AND TIPS

In this final section, I have included ten items which are tips and techniques that I have learnt over the years and also seen others use really effectively. In my view, each of these complement a Positive People Leadership style:

- Summarise and be clear
- Understand your Critical Success Factors
- Walking one-to-ones
- Rotate the chair
- In a complex, fast-moving situation, take quick decisions
- Overinvest at the beginning
- Don't put off difficult tasks
- Ask for one-page summaries
- Create a brilliant working environment
- Pause for five seconds and reflect

It is so easy to hold a meeting where lots gets discussed and it feels like a really useful session, but at the end of it, everyone leaves the meeting, and nothing happens. Sound familiar? There are lots of tips for running effective meetings, starting with a clear agenda, purpose and good etiquette. But most fundamental is taking the time to summarise the discussion, confirm specific decisions and actions. Basic but, amazingly, often poorly executed.

I once worked for a leader who was incredibly quick at taking decisions. Initially, I found this unsettling, but the environment we were operating in was very complex and dynamic – several companies like ours were all competing to be first to market to launch an innovative product. The valuable lesson I learnt at that time was not to overanalyse in this type of situation, where there were just too many variables, and speed was the most important factor. By making a series of decisions quickly, at each step we had a different perspective and could quickly assess whether the decision had worked and use this knowledge to reverse it if necessary. All while our competitors were still thinking about what to do. Not always appropriate but definitely an agile way of working.

Many years ago, I went to visit one of my suppliers who were based at a very old manufacturing site. I remember being asked to sit in a shabby waiting room, before being escorted across a yard to offices with faded carpets, drab walls and full of very tired furniture. Utterly sad and depressing and energy-draining. How easy it would have been for the leaders to freshen the place up, install new carpets and desks, put some colourful posters on the walls, replace offices with an open plan layout, install a table tennis table or two and generally work with their teams to make it a fun and interesting place to work and collaborate. To create an environment to bring out the best in people.

One of the ideas I have tried out more recently is to pause for five seconds and reflect before opening my mouth. I have surprised myself with how often this has caused me to either not say something I would have regretted or simply to articulate what I wanted to say more clearly. Or, in some cases, say something far more considered and useful, different to my initial reaction. A very powerful technique.

SUMMARISE AND BE CLEAR

At the end of the discussion on a topic, or when you have completed a meeting agenda item, make sure you summarise the outcome of the discussion.

Recap specifically what was agreed:

- Any decisions made
- Any actions taken – what, who and by when

Do this for all meetings and meaningful discussions, whether it's a one-to-one or a large meeting. Or ask someone else to summarise. It's often a good idea to get the person who has taken an action to summarise it. Or the person taking the minutes. Then check for agreement. Make sure the other person or persons agree. Note it down. Then move on.

Summarise often. Summarise and be clear.

UNDERSTAND YOUR CRITICAL SUCCESS FACTORS

Whenever you start a new programme or role, spend time making sure you are really clear on the outcomes that you need to achieve.

Spend time with each of your stakeholders (your boss, your customers, workstream leads, partners) to understand clearly what it is that you have to deliver to be brilliant. And of course, how to deliver it.

Once you are clear on this and have started to build up an understanding of the role or programme, determine what your Critical Success Factors are.

Critical Success Factors (CSFs) are the key things that you will need to particularly focus on to ensure success. They may represent specific risks or threats or key components of the programme that underpin everything else. Those vital aspects of the programme that will be key to underpin the outcome.

Examples could be:

- A key programme dependency
- The performance of a specific supplier or partner
- A major deliverable or workstream
- Setting up a new partnership or transition
- Management of a major risk, such as security or compliance, with a major legal or contractual obligation
- Effective programme communication
- And so on…

Once these are clear, make sure that as a Positive People Leader, you focus on these. Set up the structure of your team or programme to take these into account, with single points of ownership within the team. Plus, use the CSFs as the basis for your reporting, key performance measures, meetings and governance.

Understanding and managing your CSFs well is key to prioritising your focus and leading your team to success.

WALKING ONE-TO-ONES

When you have an informal update scheduled with someone, consider changing the environment once in a while. Particularly if it's a regular meeting.

Go for a walk. A stroll for thirty minutes in the fresh air. Ideally somewhere quiet and beautiful. Along a river or near water is good. Through a park is also good. Especially if the weather is nice.

Free your mind from the office environment. Leave it behind and enjoy the fresh air. And focus on the person you are with. Have a rich conversation.

Prepare beforehand any key points you want to cover and make sure they do the same (this is always good, basic meeting preparation). And let them know you intend to make this meeting a walking meeting; make sure that they are ok with it.

Ensure that one of you agrees to summarise the key agreements/decisions/actions by email afterwards.

Try a walking one-to-one occasionally and freshen up your catch-up meetings.

ROTATE THE CHAIR

You don't need to always chair your team meetings. Get everyone to take it in turns.

Make sure each person is clear what that means. The chair is accountable for ensuring that the meeting is well prepared, the agenda is set and the right people attend. During the meeting, they are responsible for the smooth running of the session, in particular:

- That the meeting outcomes are agreed and achieved
- Making sure everyone is heard/has their say
- That decisions and actions are clear
- Keeping it to time

It's great experience for everyone to take a turn at this and your team meeting is an ideal place to try this out. It adds value to your team, plus you have the benefit when you are not chairing the meeting of being able to give extra focus to the discussion.

At the end of the meeting, each chairperson should briefly ask for feedback on how the meeting went –

quick round-the-table comments to enable continuous improvement, both for the chair and participants.

Set the example yourself of how to chair meetings well, but also be prepared to learn from your team. You may be surprised at how much better some of your team members are at this than you.

Try rotating the chair in your team meetings.

IN A COMPLEX, FAST-MOVING SITUATION, TAKE QUICK DECISIONS

In a highly complex and fast-moving environment, it often does not pay to spend ages overanalysing the situation before you make a choice. Otherwise, you may find that by the time you think you are ready to make a choice, something has changed, and you have to start your assessment all over again and are paralysed by your analysis, never able to commit to a decision before events overtake you. There are just too many variables.

In these situations, it is often better to do a rapid assessment with the inputs that you have, then make a quick decision, to go with your gut. Then quickly assess the impact. And if necessary, make another decision, a course correction, even reversing the decision if you need to.

The key point is that having made a decision, you will have much more information than if you were still waiting.

If it's the right decision, that's great. If it's not right, you will know and can do something about it quickly.

You have to use your judgement as to when it is appropriate to apply this approach. It can work really well in rapidly growing new markets, where a series of quick decisions with fast feedback between each decision can leave slower competitors way behind.

OVERINVEST AT THE

BEGINNING

The beginning of something new is the most important phase. A new project. A new customer. A new delivery partnership. A new starter in your team. These are times to overinvest.

Overinvest in a new project with time, energy and experts. Get it set up well with the right people, a solid plan, good governance, clear and definite outcomes. Start with everything clearly established and under control and it will run well.

Overinvest in getting to know customers and partners from the outset of your relationship. Set clear expectations: upfront commitments on how you will work together and what good looks like.

Make new starters welcome. Ensure their first days and weeks are memorable. That they have support from you and others. That they are set up to succeed.

Overinvest at the beginning and set things up well. Spend effort and energy at the outset to grow successful outcomes and they will need less of your time later. It takes ten times more effort to recover a project or a relationship than it does to put the extra effort in to set it up right at the start.

DON'T PUT OFF
DIFFICULT TASKS

It's so easy to procrastinate when you have a difficult task to implement. When you have made up your mind and know it's the right thing to do, but it's not going to be easy. A hard decision that affects people. Such as:

- To reorganise the team, change roles, create redundancies
- To remove someone with the wrong behaviours
- Something that will be unpopular with many people

But once you have thought through the situation and come to a decision, and know it is the right thing to do, do it. And do it quickly. Do it right. Have a solid and professional plan to implement. Be human; be compassionate. Be sure to communicate your reasons clearly. Act with utmost integrity and respect – always.

If you don't implement difficult tasks quickly, the situation rarely goes away. Usually, it just gets worse and becomes more difficult.

Don't put off difficult actions.

ASK FOR ONE-PAGE

SUMMARIES

One of my favourite quotes is: 'If you can't explain it simply, you don't understand it well enough'. This is attributed to Albert Einstein and is a brilliant statement.

It is amazing how things can become unnecessarily complex. It is so easy to drown in data. In pages and pages of long reports, which over time grow larger and larger. But of course, you don't need to be bombarded with complex data. You need straightforward, concise and clear information.

Challenge your team to produce one-page summaries that explain all you need to know. Use this technique to eliminate large decks of PowerPoint and huge reports. Ensure that all information has a clear purpose. It will help you to keep out of unnecessary detail. And it will drive your teams to think about what the essential key points are they need to make and the most important KPIs to share. It will challenge them to ensure that they themselves really understand the key messages, rather than circulate lots of data to everyone. Ultimately, it will save everyone's time and keep focus on the important things.

Ask for quality one-page summaries. Don't accept more.

CREATE A BRILLIANT
WORKING ENVIRONMENT

Workspace is collaborative space where you come together when you need to. Now more than ever before. Homeworking and flexible working will be increasingly part of our working cycle, and the office environment needs to complement this and serve an ever more distinct function for when we need to be together.

Your office environment sets the tone for your team and needs to be totally in tune with your vision and values. Work with your team to design a place that you will enjoy working in. A place that you will want to be in, rather than have to be in. Positive People Leaders create workspaces that radiate energy, fun and productivity. They often have the following characteristics:

- Open and airy
- Brightness and light
- Clean and uncluttered
- Interesting things on the walls, such as progress against

shared goals, celebrations and call outs, pictures from social events.

- Well-being everywhere – comfy furniture, breakout areas, healthy snacks

They have a buzz about them. You can feel it and smell the passion and engagement. You will hear laughter, often. And that atmosphere doesn't change when senior managers or customers are around. The team are proud to invite them in.

Create a brilliant working environment for your team.

PAUSE FOR FIVE SECONDS
AND REFLECT

Pause for five seconds and reflect.

When someone says something that triggers you, don't launch into an immediate emotional reaction. Pause for five seconds and reflect. Give yourself time to be clear how you want to respond. Make sure your response is considered. If you react immediately, you are likely to do or say something impulsively that is not properly thought through. Which you might later regret.

It's amazing how powerful this technique is. You will surprise yourself with the number of times that after a short moment of calm, you make a more considered response. You say or do something more beneficial. More helpful and useful. More appropriate. You might just pause and do nothing. You might still take the action your emotions originally suggested to you. But it's more likely to be the right action. With increased self-awareness.

So many times, people take an impulsive action in response to a rapid emotional reaction and regret it. Pause for five seconds and reflect. Often.

SUMMARY:

TECHNIQUES AND TIPS

- At the end of each discussion you have, make it meaningful and clear by summarising the outcome, decisions and actions – who, what and by when.
- Invest time to clearly understand the Critical Success Factors for your role and your programmes that will be key to delivering your desired outcomes. Then use these as a framework to structure your team with single points of ownership and as a focus for reporting and governance.
- Freshen up your one-to-one meetings by changing the environment from time to time. Try walking in the fresh air, ideally somewhere quiet and beautiful.
- Ask your team members to help to run your team meetings. Get everyone to take it in turns to chair the meeting, including preparation and taking responsibility for the smooth running of the session.
- In highly complex and fast-moving environments, beware of overanalysing the situation and delaying

taking action. Often it is better to make a fast decision and gain better insight, then use this improved knowledge to amend or 'course-correct' the decision if necessary.

- Always overinvest at the beginning of a new project or partnership to set it up well. Invest time, energy and expertise to make sure it is built on strong foundations: clear outcomes, a solid plan and well-structured governance.
- Don't put off difficult tasks. Do them in the right way, but once you have made up your mind, do them quickly.
- Challenge your team (and yourself) to produce one-page summaries. Don't accept unnecessary detail and ensure that all information you receive has a clear purpose.
- Create a brilliant working environment that everyone wants to come together in. Use your imagination to create an interesting, fun, collaborative space that you can fill with passion and engagement.
- When someone says something that triggers you, pause for five seconds and reflect. Don't launch into an immediate emotional reaction.

ACKNOWLEDGEMENTS

I would like to thank the following people for their help with this book:

Sue Rowe for your encouragement and support.

Adam Rowe, Richard Rowe, Stephen Rowe, Becky Rowe, Eleanor Blanning and Vicky Gregory for reviewing the drafts and giving me valuable feedback.

Finally, a big thank you to all the leaders I have worked for and with over the years. Plus, everyone who has worked for me at the various stages of my continuous development journey to strive to be a better leader. I have learnt a huge amount from you all and continue to do so.